Tuning In

The Great Fire of London is written as a d[...] read from beginning to end.

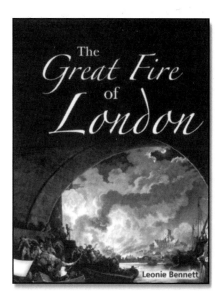

The front cover

Read the title.

What do you know about the Great Fire of London?

The back cover

Read the blurb to find out what this book is about.

Contents

How the Fire Started ... 2
The Diary of George Walker ... 4
After the Fire ... 14
Glossary ... 16

Leonie Bennett

Contents

Read the list of contents and turn to the glossary.

Speaking and Listening

Find 'diarist' and read what it means.

Can you think of another word that adds 'ist' to describe what a person does?

1

READ

Read pages 2 and 3

Purpose: to find out how the fire started and who the diarist was.

EXPLORE

Pause at page 3

Why do you think Samuel Pepys' diary is so famous?

Speaking and Listening

What does 'the rest of this book is fictional' mean?

Find 'fictional' in the glossary.

What would be another way of describing 'a shower of firedrops'?

Tricky words (page 2):
The word 'Faryner' may be beyond the children's word recognition skills. Tell this word to the children.

The word 'Pepys' may also want to be discussed as a tricky word.

How the Fire Started

On 1 September 1666 a baker called Thomas Faryner forgot to put out the fire in his oven before he went to bed. A spark jumped out and started The Great Fire of London.

Samuel Pepys, a famous **diarist**, was an **eyewitness**. This is what he wrote in his **diary** about the fire.

'It made me weep to see it. The churches, houses, and all on fire and flaming at once, and a horrid noise the flames made, and the cracking of houses at their ruin...with one's face in the wind you were almost burned with a shower of firedrops.'

The diary in the rest of this book is **fictional**. It tells us what a child might have seen and heard while London was burning.

What do **you** think it would have been like to have seen London burn?

A single spark from a baker's fire started The Great Fire of London.

This is a painting of Samuel Pepys. His diary tells us a lot about life in London during the 1600s.

2

3

READ

Read pages 4 and 5

Purpose: to find out what George Walker saw.

EXPLORE

Pause at page 5

What were two things that helped the fire to spread so quickly?

Speaking and Listening

Would you have gone into the city like George and his father if you had been told the city was on fire?

The Diary of George Walker

Sunday 2 September 1666

Father woke me early. He told me that the city was on fire and that 300 houses had already burned down!

We went out into the city. It was windy and the flames were jumping from one house to the next. It was noisy too. The roofs of houses were falling in and people were shouting. Smoke was everywhere.

This is an artist's sketch of the city of London in 1647. Many of the buildings in the picture were destroyed in the fire.

Timber houses

The houses in London had **timber frames** and **thatched** roofs, which burned very easily.

4

5

READ

Read pages 6 and 7

Purpose: to read what happened next.

EXPLORE

Pause at page 7

How long has the fire been spreading?

What is the word on page 6 that we don't use often now? (*nighshirts*)

Before looking up 'firebreak' in the glossary, can you work out from the text what it means?

Speaking and Listening

Do you think George's father is right about their house?

Tricky word (page 6):
The word 'possessions' may be beyond the children's word recognition skills. Tell this word to the children.

Monday 3 September 1666

Today the streets were crowded.

I saw people in their **nightshirts** running away from their blazing homes. Some people were pushing carts piled high with all their **possessions**. I even saw a sick person being carried down the street in his bed.

We went to the river. People were jumping onto boats to get away from the flames. We live a little way out of the city and father says our house will be safe.

Fighting the fire

The king's men pulled down houses to make a gap called a **firebreak**. This stopped the fire passing from one house to another.

6

7

READ

Read pages 8 and 9

Purpose: to find out if George's house is saved.

EXPLORE

Pause at page 9

What possessions has George's father buried?

Why did he not take them away?

Speaking and Listening

Do you think people would behave the same way today if there was a fire?

What would you save from your house?

Tricky word (page 8):
The word 'jewellery' may be beyond the children's word recognition skills. Tell this word to the children.

Tuesday 4 September 1666

Father says that the fire might reach our house after all. He has dug a big hole in the garden and buried mother's jewellery, some fine wine and the silver candlesticks.

Our neighbours have taken as many of their things as they could carry and have gone into the country.

Soldiers are now using **gunpowder** to blow up houses to make firebreaks.

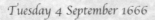
What would **you** save from your house?

This is a painting of The Great Fire of London. It shows people escaping from burning houses with their belongings.

READ

Read pages 10 and 11

Purpose: to read how the people tried to put out the fire.

EXPLORE

Pause at page 11

Who would put out a fire today?

Who put out fires in 1666?

Speaking and Listening

What is a squirt? Is it in the glossary?

Tricky word (page 10):
The word 'squirts' may be beyond the children's word recognition skills. Tell this word to the children.

Wednesday 5 September 1666

Today I watched people pouring buckets of water on the fires. There are very few places to get water from in the city. After the long hot summer, even the river is low.

Many people have taken their possessions to the churches. They are made of stone and will not burn like the wooden houses.

Mother says that the fire will stop spreading now because the wind has dropped.

There was no fire brigade. People had buckets, **squirts** and long hooks to pull the thatch off burning houses.

Which materials burn slowly? Which materials burn quickly?

wood • stone
metal • paper

The people in this picture are putting out the fire with a squirt.

10

11

READ

Read pages 12 and 13

Purpose: to find out if George's house was burnt.

EXPLORE

Pause at page 13

How long did the fire last?

Speaking and Listening

Are there fires today that last for days?

How many people did you expect to die in the fire?

Thursday 6 September 1666

This morning there is no wind. At last, the fire is over.

Many buildings have been burned to the ground. In many places the ground is too hot to walk on.

My cousins have come to live with us. They have lost their house, their money and their clothes. Many people are living in tents in the fields outside the city.

Father says we are all lucky to be alive.

Many people lost their homes in the fire. They made tents out of any materials they could find.

This is a map of London after the fire. The area in white shows buildings that were destroyed in the fire.

Great Fire deaths
Only five people died in The Great Fire of London.

12

13

READ

Read pages 14 and 15

Purpose: to read how London was rebuilt.

EXPLORE

Pause at page 15

What were the major changes made when London was rebuilt?

Speaking and Listening

Do you think everything was rebuilt after the fire?

After the Fire

After the fire people needed new homes. The new houses were made of brick and the new streets were wider.

Lots of churches and St Paul's **Cathedral** were re-built by Sir Christopher Wren. You can still see his churches in London today.

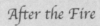
Why do you think the fire was called 'The Great Fire of London'?

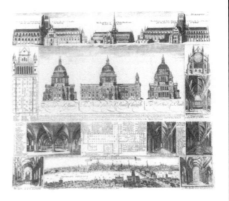

These are Sir Christopher Wren's sketches of St Paul's Cathedral and other buildings. The three drawings in the middle are of St. Paul's.

Lost in the fire

The fire destroyed:

- 13,200 houses
- St Paul's Cathedral
- 87 churches
- 3 city gates
- 4 stone bridges

READ

Read page 16

Purpose: to find out the purpose of a glossary.

EXPLORE

Pause at page 16

Read the words in bold.

What do you notice about how they are listed?

Why have those words been chosen for the glossary?

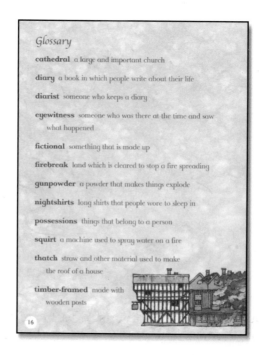

Glossary

cathedral a large and important church

diary a book in which people write about their life

diarist someone who keeps a diary

eyewitness someone who was there at the time and saw what happened

fictional something that is made up

firebreak land which is cleared to stop a fire spreading

gunpowder a powder that makes things explode

nightshirts long shirts that people wore to sleep in

possessions things that belong to a person

squirt a machine used to spray water on a fire

thatch straw and other material used to make the roof of a house

timber-framed made with wooden posts

16